A LETTER FROM PETER MUNK

Since we started the Munk Debates, my wife, Melanie, and I have been deeply gratified at how quickly they have captured the public's imagination. From the time of our first event in May 2008, we have hosted what I believe are some of the most exciting public policy debates in Canada and internationally. Global in focus, the Munk Debates have tackled a range of issues, such as humanitarian intervention, the effectiveness of foreign aid, the threat of global warming, religion's impact on geopolitics, the rise of China, and the decline of Europe. These compelling topics have served as intellectual and ethical grist for some of the world's most important thinkers and doers, from Henry Kissinger to Tony Blair, Christopher Hitchens to Paul Krugman, Peter Mandelson to Fareed Zakaria.

The issues raised at the Munk Debates have not only fostered public awareness, but they have also helped many of us become more involved and, therefore, less intimidated by the concept of globalization. It is so easy to be inward-looking. It is so easy to be xenophobic. It is so easy to be nationalistic. It is hard to go into the unknown. Globalization, for many people, is an abstract concept at best. The purpose of this debate series is to help people feel more familiar with our fast-changing world and more comfortable participating in the universal dialogue about the issues and events that will shape our collective future.

I don't need to tell you that there are many, many burning issues. Global warming, the plight of extreme poverty, genocide, or our shaky financial order: these are just a few of the critical issues that matter to people. And it seems to me, and to my foundation board members, that the quality of the public dialogue on these critical issues diminishes in direct proportion to the salience and number of these issues clamouring for our attention. By trying to highlight the most important issues at crucial moments in the global conversation, these debates not only profile the ideas and opinions of some of the world's brightest thinkers, but they also crystallize public passion and knowledge, helping to tackle some of the challenges confronting humankind.

I have learned in life — and I'm sure many of you will share this view — that challenges bring out the best in us. I hope you'll agree that the participants in these debates challenge not only each other but also each of us to think clearly and logically about important problems facing our world.

Peter Munk
Founder, Aurea Foundation
Toronto, Ontario

THE GLOBAL REFUGEE CRISIS: HOW SHOULD WE RESPOND?

ARBOUR AND SCHAMA VS. FARAGE AND STEYN

THE MUNK DEBATES

Edited by Rudyard Griffiths

ANANSI

This edition published in 2016 by
House of Anansi Press Inc.
www.houseofanansi.com

House of Anansi Press is committed to protecting our natural environment.
As part of our efforts, the interior of this book is printed on paper that contains
100% post-consumer recycled fibres, is acid-free, and is processed chlorine-free.

20 19 18 17 16   1 2 3 4 5

Library and Archives Canada Cataloguing in Publication

The global refugee crisis : how should we respond?
/ Arbour and Schama vs. Farage and Steyn ; edited by Rudyard
Griffiths.

(The Munk debates)
Issued in print and electronic formats.
ISBN 978-1-4870-0212-1 (paperback).—ISBN 978-1-4870-0213-8
(html)

1. Refuge (Humanitarian assistance). 2. Refugees—
International cooperation. 3. Syria—History—Civil War, 2011– —
Refugees. I. Arbour, Louise, 1947–, panelist II. Schama, Simon,
panelist III. Griffiths, Rudyard, editor IV. Steyn, Mark, 1959–,
panelist V. Farage, Nigel, 1964–, panelist VI. Series: Munk debates

HV640.G56 2016   362.87   C2016-903819-X
                   C2016-903820-3
Library of Congress Control Number: 20169429 78

Cover design: Alysia Shewchuk
Typesetting: Alysia Shewchuk
Transcription: Transcript Divas

 Canada Council
for the Arts
Conseil des Arts
du Canada
 ONTARIO ARTS COUNCIL
CONSEIL DES ARTS DE L'ONTARIO
an Ontario government agency
un organisme du gouvernement de l'Ontario

*We acknowledge for their financial support of our publishing program
the Canada Council for the Arts, the Ontario Arts Council, and the Government of
Canada through the Canada Book Fund.*

Printed and bound in Canada

MIX
Paper from
responsible sources
FSC® C004071

CONTENTS

The Global Refugee Crisis:
How Should We Respond?

Pro: Louise Arbour and Simon Schama
Con: Nigel Farage and Mark Steyn

April 1, 2016
Toronto, Ontario

THE GLOBAL REFUGEE CRISIS:
HOW SHOULD WE RESPOND?

RUDYARD GRIFFITHS: Ladies and gentlemen, welcome to the Munk Debate on the global refugee crisis. My name is Rudyard Griffiths and I have the privilege of organizing this semi-annual debate series and, once again, serving as your moderator.

I want to begin tonight's proceedings by welcoming the North America–wide TV audience that is tuning in to this debate right now across Canada from coast to coast to coast on CPAC, Canada's Public Affairs Channel, and across the continental United States on C-SPAN. It's the first time the Munk Debate has been live throughout the continent of North America and it's terrific to have that viewing audience joining us this evening.

A warm hello also to our online audience. They're logging onto this debate right now on our website, www.munkdebates.com. It's great to have you as virtual participants in tonight's proceedings.

And finally, hello to you, the more than three thousand people who've once again filled Roy Thomson Hall on a Friday night to capacity for yet another Munk Debate. All of us associated with the Aurea Foundation thank you for supporting the simple idea that this debate series is dedicated to: more and better public debates. So, bravo, ladies and gentlemen. Thank you for being part of tonight's conversation.

Our ability to continue these debates year after year, and to bring some of the world's sharpest minds and brightest thinkers here to the stage, would not be possible without the generosity, the foresight, and the creativity of our hosts tonight. Please join me in a warm appreciation of the Aurea Foundation and its founders, Peter and Melanie Munk.

It's the moment we've been waiting for. Let's get our two teams of debaters out here centre stage and our debate underway. Our resolution tonight is taken from the inscription on the Statue of Liberty, "Be it resolved: Give us your tired, your poor, your huddled masses yearning to breathe free."

Please welcome our first speaker in support of the resolution. She's a former Canadian Supreme Court justice, chief prosecutor of the International Criminal Tribunals for Yugoslavia and Rwanda, and the United Nations High Commissioner for Human Rights (UNHCR), among many other accomplishments. Ladies and gentlemen, please welcome Canada's Louise Arbour.

Louise's teammate is the internationally acclaimed historian, cultural commentator, and art critic Simon Schama. Please come out on stage, Simon.

Well, one great team of debaters deserves another. Speaking against the resolution, "Be it resolved: Give us your tired, your poor, your huddled masses yearning to breathe free," is the renowned columnist, author, and conservative human rights activist Mark Steyn.

Mark's debating partner is the leader of UKIP, the United Kingdom Independence Party, and a member of the European Parliament. He's here tonight from the United Kingdom. Under his leadership, UKIP won almost four million votes in the 2015 national election. Ladies and gentlemen, Nigel Farage.

Before our debate begins, I need your help with a last-minute housekeeping item: our countdown clock, an invention we *love* at the Munk Debates. It keeps us on schedule and our debaters on their toes. When you see these clocks reach their final moments, join me in a round of applause that will let our debaters know that their time is up. We had Henry Kissinger up here once and he didn't think his time was up . . . but I digress. I don't think any of our debaters will make the same mistake.

Now, this is the part I enjoy most. We asked all of you here tonight to vote on the resolution on your way in. You were asked, "Do you support or oppose the motion, 'Be it resolved: give us your tired, your poor, your huddled masses yearning to breathe free'?" The results are interesting: 77 percent of you agree, and 23 percent disagree.

To give a sense of how much this debate is in play, we asked: "Depending on what you hear during the debate, are you open to changing your votes?" Let's see that result. Wow: 79 percent of you were open to changing your votes. Only 21 percent of you are committed to your viewpoint. This debate is very much in play; either side can take it.

Let's go to our opening statements. I'd like six minutes on the clock for each of our debaters. Ms. Arbour, your six minutes begins now.

LOUISE ARBOUR: Thank you very much. Good evening, ladies and gentlemen. The words of the motion that I'm here to support were written by a woman, Emma Lazarus, and these words are engraved on a famous statute of a woman holding a torch, and maybe less noticeably holding also the tablets of law with a broken chain at her feet. So it should come as no surprise to you that this has consider-able appeal to me. But don't let that fool you. This is not a sentimental call for do-gooders to unite, nor a romantic projection of what the new world is going to be all about.

Understood in today's terms, it's a moving, poetic way of capturing both the spirit and the letter of the 1951 Refugee Convention. It was written essentially because of and for Europe, and it remains the framework within which a world purporting to be governed by the rule of law must deal with the current refugee crisis in Europe and must also stop turning a blind eye to equally pressing crises elsewhere — in South Sudan, for instance. This is part of the "Never again!" that the world screamed loud and clear after the Holocaust and has betrayed on so many occasions since then. Today should not be one of those.

I want to look at this issue both from a Canadian and international perspective. The international framework is very clear. Virtually all of the countries concerned with the current flow of refugees fleeing the war-torn countries of Syria, Iraq, Afghanistan, Somalia, and Libya are parties to the Refugee Convention, and they are obligated to grant asylum to those fleeing political and other forms of persecution. The protection framework that is set in place by the convention outlines that refugees should not be penalized for their illegal entry or stay in a country. The reverse would obviously be a way to completely emasculate the right of asylum, and the principle of non-refoulement precludes returning refugees to countries where they are at risk. This puts a disproportionate demand on countries that are more easily reachable than others. In the case of Syria, the neighbouring countries of Lebanon, Jordan, and Turkey currently have some 4.5 million Syrian refugees, and the countries that are at the external borders of Europe — Greece, Italy, and so on — are also seeing a large influx.

This leads to another fundamental principle that underpins the Refugee Convention: the need for international co-operation and burden sharing, and I'm cautious here about using the word *burden*. Now I want to mention Canada. We often define ourselves by our geography, and on this issue our geography is relevant. The nature of our borders is such that we are virtually immune from a flow of asylum seekers arriving on our soil by land or sea — although, the result of the upcoming American elections may change that! We'll cross that bridge when we get there. As a result, I believe we have a special obligation to provide for a generous resettlement program aiming both at welcoming refugees and at easing the burden on states that are struggling to live up to their international obligations. And I believe that with true international co-operation in place, this is eminently feasible. We should do it the smart way by ensuring that asylum seekers can travel safely to places of refuge, thereby undercutting the smugglers, and by deploying extraordinary resources to meet this extraordinary challenge.

I am aware of the fear that an influx of foreigners will transform our social fabric in an undesirable way, but the reality is that our social fabric is changing anyway in this increasingly interconnected world. We have a choice. We can look to the past and stagnate in isolation, or we can embrace a future in which our children will develop their own culture fully open to that of others, inspired by the choices that we are making today. The greatest threat to Western values is not an influx of people who may not share those values today; it's the hypocrisy of those claiming to protect these values and then repudiating them by their actions.

I expect that we're going to hear tonight that Muslims are different, that they pose a unique, novel, and existential threat to our democracies. Not only has this been the ugly response to just about every wave of new immigrants in history, but, ironically, it plays right into the hands of the violent jihadist groups that are attacking us. These violent groups have a political, not a religious agenda. They seek to destroy our democracies not by infiltrating or taking over our institutions but by letting us slowly self-implode in response to the fear that risks turning us against ourselves, thereby destroying the very key features of our open society. We need to be smarter than that, and we need to welcome people who, like all of us who came from somewhere else at some point, will build an ever-evolving free and strong Canada. Thank you very much.

RUDYARD GRIFFITHS: With time still on the clock. Mark Steyn, you're up next. Your six minutes begins now.

MARK STEYN: Madame Arbour described a refugee situation that is not happening in Europe at the moment. The great question before us tonight is whether the "huddled masses" on those "teeming shores" are really "yearning to breathe free," or whether they're simply economic migrants who want to avail themselves of the comforts of advanced societies. There are three thousand people here in Roy Thomson Hall tonight. It would nice if everyone who lived in Toronto could be in Roy Thomson Hall right now, but if everyone in Toronto moves into Roy Thomson Hall, it isn't Roy Thomson Hall anymore. And that's the situation facing Europe today.

The people who have entered Europe are not refugees as the term has traditionally been understood and as Madame Arbour explained in terms of the Geneva Convention. In Europe in 2015, men represented 77 percent of the asylum applications — that's an extraordinary population deformation. In most civil wars, this is the demographic that would be back home fighting for their country. It's as if, during the American Revolution, General Washington and the rest of the chaps had gone off to France and left Martha and the other women and children back home to fend for themselves.

What does it mean to breathe free? Under the Taliban, it's illegal for Madame Arbour to feel sunlight on her face. It's literally a crime for her to "breathe free." She can breathe only through a mask approved by the man who owns her, in effect. So what happens when you put a man from that kind of society in, say, a Scandinavian town? Northern Europe has enjoyed a culture of mixed public bathing since the nineteenth century, but a benign social activity to Germans and Scandinavians is something entirely different to men from a culture where women are chattel. Female patrons of public baths are now routinely assaulted. And in January, Sweden's national swimming arena was forced to segregate men and women in the hot tubs for the first time. Goodbye to a century-old tradition; migrant rights trump your culture.

Our response is, "Oh, they come from a different culture; they don't know that you're not meant to grope women's breasts." In Germany they put up pictograms with a breast and a groping hand with a red X through it. Last month, a mere fortnight after acing a training course on how to treat women with respect, a fifteen-year-old Afghan dragged a caterer at a Belgian refugee centre into the basement and raped her. We'll say that the course on treating women with respect needs some fine-tuning. We'll get better pictograms. But in the meantime, migrant rights trump women's rights.

Madame Arbour was the first prosecutor ever to charge rape as a crime against humanity. In 2007 she published an important report on the use of rape in Sudan as a weapon of war. It was a distressing report. She documented fifteen individual cases of sexual assault, including rape, in victims as young as fourteen. If Madame Arbour were to publish a similar report on Germany today, she'd be able to cite more than five hundred cases from just one night in just one town — Cologne — on New Year's Eve. Victims were as young as three. Think about that: a three-year-old was raped by a migrant. A seven-year-old was gang-raped by five migrants in Hamburg just a few days ago. On Wednesday, a schoolgirl was gang-raped on the ferry from Sweden to Finland. Migrant rights now trump children's rights. What a pity Madame Arbour's successor at the UN isn't interested in producing a report on that rape epidemic.

The police chief of Vienna has advised women that it's no longer safe to go out unaccompanied. Migrant rights trump the right to freedom of movement. It's easy to shrug — "Oh, well, it's just a few disabled kids, just anecdotes." Forget the anecdotes and run the numbers. In Europe, unaccompanied minors are 90 percent male, which means that in one year, Swedish adolescents now have a more distorted sex differential than China does after thirty years of its totalitarian one-child policy. In China there are 119 boys for every girl. Among Swedish adolescents, it is now 123 boys for every girl, just from last year's immigration. That's a fact. I hope tonight we'll put aside the sentimentalism that often imbues this subject and stick with the facts.

Madame Arbour said some things that I agree with. She recently said, "Why are we always talking about the danger that these people will transform us? They may transform us for the better." So she and I agree that immigration on this scale is transformative. The only difference is that Madame Arbour thinks it's for the better and I don't. I'm genuinely curious to know what aspects of Afghan and Syrian and Sudanese culture she would like us to be transformed by: Women's rights? Fast-track justice whereby gays get thrown off rooftops? Polygamy? Child brides? Clitoridectomies? The bracing commitment to free speech? I would like an answer on that from Madame Arbour tonight. Thank you very much.

RUDYARD GRIFFITHS: Simon Schama, over to you.

SIMON SCHAMA: Well, I'm going to start by saying, "Oh Canada, your borders are safe." I can tell you why. I was asked this morning at the Toronto airport what I was doing here, and I said, "Well, I've come to talk about refugees and migrants," and I was immediately taken off for secondary screening. So it's not only dangerous to talk about it; it's dangerous to be known to be talking about it.

The words in our resolution tonight were written by Emma Lazarus. She was a Sephardic Jewess and a wealthy woman in New York. She wrote them in 1883 after looking at the victims of Russian pogroms who had come to America having suffered horrendous atrocities in Kishinev, Odessa, and Elisavetgrad. She saw them on Wards Island, and she didn't make the distinction that they were economic migrants. By the way, Mark, your number is wrong. It's not 77 percent; we know from United Nations agencies that the figure is 61 percent, and that's significant. This is an uninterrupted moment, Mark; we'll have rebuttal time afterwards. I know radio hosts don't usually like that, but that's the case.

She did that because when you are fleeing from a place of cruelty and atrocity and your house has been blown up, your whole possibility of livelihood's been taken away from you, and your children have no food, no medicine, what are you exactly? You're terrifyingly running away from catastrophe, and vast numbers of Syrians are displaced — four million of them internally displaced. So those who are escaping the hell of Libya and Somalia and Afghanistan are fleeing exactly the monsters of Islamofascism that Mark accurately describes. They're not their friends. They're not their secret co-conspirators. They are horrified. They're trying to get away from that culture.

Now, it's fine to say, "Well, in those days . . ." And as some of you know, the reason why the lines from Emma Lazarus's "The New Colossus" were not immediately put on the Statue of Liberty — they were only put there in 1903 as a result of the efforts of her friend Georgina Schuyler — was because of a ferocious agitation on the part of some people at the immigration restriction league and its British equivalent, called the British Brothers'

League. These groups said the unwashed, the filthy, those who do not share our language, our religion, our values would destroy the white race. Madison Grant wrote a book called *The Passing of the Great Race*. Tom Watson, the populist, described the millions of distressed as the scum of creation. Nonetheless, the United States, as an honour to its tradition set out in Crèvecoeur's "What Is an American" in 1782, admitted five million of those refugees between 1880 and 1890.

And the argument will be made that in those days democracy was more confident. I agree with you absolutely about that. It was. It was more articulate. It was less offensive. It was more forthright. And besides, you may say, people coming from eastern Europe or central Europe did not bear democracy the grudge; they didn't want to overthrow it. Yes, they did. Yes, they did. Those teeming millions that Emma Lazarus emotionally described were full of anarchists and communists dedicated to the overthrow of capitalism. But liberal capitalism was strong enough to let them in anyway, and as a result, the American Republic and Great Britain thrived and flourished and prospered, and my own grandparents were among those who had Britain to thank for that more expansive view of what democracy could accommodate.

Right now, we're talking about a drop in the ocean, really. There are one billion of us in Europe and Canada and the United States. We're talking about 20,000 refugees being admitted to Britain. We're talking about 100,000 refugees in the United States proposed by the president, of whom only 25,000 will come from Syria.

Are they all ravening sexual monsters of Mark Steyn's X-rated horror?

Muslims are not all Salafists. And not all Salafists are jihadists either. There are quieter Salafists. Do Salafist jihadists pose a mortal threat? You bet your life they do. There is a real war of that kind going on, but what should we do to resist the poison of apocalyptic millenarians?

The answer is not to demonize all Muslims but to engage with them. And we say, "Well, who are we engaging with? There are no Muslims who really want to stand up." That is not true. After the attack both in Paris and Brussels, 150 imams in New York got up and made a statement about the abhorrence of the act. There are even Koranic scholars, the greatest of whom is Javed Ahmad Ghamidi — if you don't know his work look it up — who are absolutely dedicated to denouncing jihadism as a perversion of the Koran.

And I just want to say that it can't possibly be true that you can't have a pluralist Muslim adoption of Western norms. In Britain, Nigel, we lived with that for years and years before jihadism became the monstrosity that it is now. My green grocer is a Kurdish Muslim. We turn on the radio in the morning and you hear Razia Iqbal through the BBC. My local newsagent tells me when to look at the *Jewish Chronicle*, and his name is Ahmed.

RUDYARD GRIFFITHS: Nigel.

NIGEL FARAGE: Good evening, everybody. If we're going to discuss the global refugee crisis, we'd better use the European Union (EU) as a case study. But first we must start by asking ourselves: What is a refugee? Now, I speak here today as the child of a family of refugees. We were French Protestants being burned at the stake for our political opinions — something many in Westminster would perhaps like to bring back today. There is no country in Europe that needs lectures about looking after refugees. But I come from a country that has, I think, done it better than anybody else. The Brits have done it with Jewish people. We've done it with Ugandan Asians. But what is a refugee? According to this 1951 convention that we talked about earlier, it's a person with a well-founded fear of persecution because of race, religion, political opinions, or orientation, who is outside their own country and fears returning to it.

I know it's tempting to support this motion. It sounds wonderful — "Give us your poor, your weak, your huddled masses" — and in doing so we can perhaps feel a sense of our own moral superiority. But just look where that idea has got the EU in the course of the last year. Jean-Claude Juncker, the unelected European Commission president who, I have to say after a good lunch, is rather fun to be with — particularly if I've been with him, actually — has changed the definition of what a refugee is to include people who come from war-torn areas. Given that the United Nations High Commissioner for Refugees says there are currently fifty-nine million people displaced in the world, that's quite a big number. But Juncker has taken an even broader definition. He said that you could qualify as a European refugee if you come from extreme poverty, which would mean three billion people could potentially come to Europe.

All of this was massively compounded by Chancellor Angela Merkel, who effectively did say "give us your weak and your poor and your huddled masses" in what I think has proved to be the worst foreign policy decision in Europe since 1945. In my view, her moral superiority was based on a level of war guilt that still exists in Germany. But she opened up the doors and a million people came in last year. But virtually none of them would qualify as refugees on any classical definition. And in fact, most of them were somewhat aggressive young males who, when they arrived and got through the border, punched the air and chanted like football supporters.

I remember as a young man watching the BBC and seeing Ugandan Asians landing on the tarmac at Heathrow, humbled, thankful, and promising that they would repay the debt Britain had shown them by integrating and becoming part of our society. Sadly, that is not what has happened in this case.

Nobody on this side of the argument is trying to say that Islam is bad or that all Muslims are bad. But what we are saying is that if you allow a very large number of young males to come to European countries, and if they come from a culture where women are at best second-class citizens, don't be surprised to see abominations such as the one we saw outside the Cologne train station on New Year's Eve. And don't be surprised that the formerly rather sleepy Swedish city of Malmö has now become the rape capital of Europe.

But that is nothing compared to what the boss of Europol said three weeks ago. He said there are now five thousand jihadi fighters, every one of them potentially a terrorist, who have got into Europe through the Greek islands posing as migrants. When the Islamic State of Iraq and the Levant (ISIL) says they will use the migrant routes to destroy the civilization of Europe, I suggest we start to take them seriously. And the difference between what is going on now and any other either migratory or refugee wave in the history of humankind that I can see is that never before have we had a fifth column — albeit a small one, thank God — but a fifth column living within our own communities that hates us, wants to kill us, and wants to completely overturn our way of life.

I believe that we in the West should give people refugee status. Throughout this whole tragedy in the Middle East and North Africa, not one person in a serious level of politics has dared to speak up for the Christians — the Christians in Iraq and the Christians in Syria, who are now only 10 percent of what they were just a few years ago. They qualify for refugee status because they're being persecuted for who they are.

We have to oppose this motion, which is at best impractical and at worst poses a threat to our entire way of life. I want us to have a proper processing mechanism. I want us to do all the things we've done, as Brits particularly, over centuries. I want us to welcome genuine refugees, not the disaster that is engulfing much of Europe today. Thank you.

RUDYARD GRIFFITHS: Thank you to the group for the very strong opening statements. We're now going to go into timed rebuttal so we can get some quick reaction from each team.

Ms. Arbour, we'll put two minutes on the clock for you. Give us your reaction to what you've heard from the other side.

LOUISE ARBOUR: All right. I have two issues. First, on the definition of refugees. I think in the current climate of warfare and armed conflict, virtually every civilian that is not a combatant qualifies for refugee protection, unless he is excluded by the convention as a war criminal. The reality is that civilian protection in armed conflict is currently non-existent. They are targeted by all sides and therefore qualify for refugee protection, for the most part.

As for the suggestion that these waves of young men coming into Europe are all economic migrants: frankly, it is hard to believe why these economic migrants would have paid thousands of dollars for the privilege of drowning in the Mediterranean, but that's another issue.

I see the clock running out so let me just address very briefly something that I hope we'll have an opportunity to return to later — the issues raised by these new-born feminists over there. I can assure you that for those of us feminists — certainly the women of my generation — who came from a cultural and political environment in this country in which religion dictated most of our rights and privileges, we've managed to start occupying our place in public life not by pushing and trying to exclude others, and certainly not by espousing as champions people who have that kind of ideology.

RUDYARD GRIFFITHS: I want to hear from the "pro" team back to back. Simon, let's have your rebuttal, and then I'll move on to Mark and Nigel.

SIMON SCHAMA: I'm struck by how obsessed with sex these two guys are. It's a bit sad, really. I just want to make the point that if you really think about the places — Afghanistan, for example, or Libya, or, of course, Syria — where most of the migrants are coming from, it's extraordinary to think that they're really just interested in a moment of possible upward social mobility. Those are all desperately brutalized, collapsing states in which there seems to be no possibility of normal life. And I dispute those figures about the 77 percent they are claiming. Why would you pursue this if you actually aren't a family in terrible distress? As Louise mentioned, haven't we all seen the dinghies and rubber crafts full of children as well as their elder brothers and fathers? Families are desperately trying to make it, often at the cost of their own lives.

But suppose that of the people who are coming over more than half are males. It would fit with the fact that more than half of those people in displaced horrible camps — like Atmeh, in Syria, where fifty-eight thousand people are stuck with desperate shortages of food and medicine and no sanitation — are men, and it would be logical to send your brothers and uncles out to sea. That's how it was, actually, in the 1880s and 1890s. And all of those men arriving weren't arriving with a purpose of upping their rape score either.

RUDYARD GRIFFITHS: Okay. Simon, we have lots of time in the cross-examination to get into these issues, so I want to come over to the other side. Mark Steyn, can we get your quick reaction to what you've heard?

MARK STEYN: I made a decision tonight that I wasn't going to do funny stuff, that I was going to be deadly serious. I'm slightly amazed at our colleagues' ability to get big laughs on gang rape. Madame Arbour talks of the newfound feminists over here. I'm not much of a feminist, but I draw the line at a three-year-old getting raped and a seven-year-old getting gang-raped in a basement. Simon tells us that, oh, we're — funnily enough — all obsessed with sex. Maybe we're not getting enough action at the Toronto singles bars! Madame Arbour, as she said, is a feminist of a certain generation, and those feminists were very clear that rape is not about sex, which she said in regards to Sudan. Whatever Simon may say, rape is about power, which is what Madame Arbour said. Here's a random example from the ten days of German migrant crimes in January: a sixteen-year-old boy was raped inside the Wolfsburg city hall; a thirteen-year-old girl was sexually assaulted near a railway station in Ellwangen; three girls were sexually assaulted at a swimming pool in Ansbach; a fifteen-year-old girl was raped at a railway station in Wuppertal; there was an attempted gang rape of a thirteen-year-old girl in Gelsenkirchen. I can go on and on. These are all rapes — gang rapes in public places, trains, streets, parks, and even city hall. And I congratulate you on getting big laughs with that — Simon, and Louise — because if

I'd known that, I'd be doing open mic on gang rape at a comedy club. It isn't funny! It isn't funny!

RUDYARD GRIFFITHS: Okay, Mark. We'll be able to get into this later. Your time is up.

MARK STEYN: And it gets to the heart of the question —

RUDYARD GRIFFITHS: You're going to have to sit down, Mark. We'll get into it in the moderated cross-examination. Nigel, you're up next for your rebuttal.

NIGEL FARAGE: Thank you. What Mark has just said is difficult to listen to, and we'd all rather pretend it isn't happening, but sadly it *is* happening. Simon, you're in denial. I'll tell you what's sad. What's sad, and you'd know as a historian, is that a hundred years ago women went into factories, earned their first decent pay packets, went to the pub, and got the vote. We've lived through a hundred years of female liberation and emancipation, and now we have the mayors of towns in Germany and in Sweden and in other parts of northern Europe telling women not to walk out after dark on their own. And in the wake of the Cologne sex attacks, the mayor of that city said to those women they really ought to dress and behave differently in public. That, Simon, is what is sad — the sheer hypocrisy of those of you that have stood up and said you're going to defend female rights when you actually think migrant rights are more important than female rights in your own community. Frankly, shame on you!

And, Louise: you're trying to redefine the 1951 convention on refugee status, but can I just challenge you to something? You know, maybe, just maybe, you would agree with me that the Australians got it right when faced with a similar problem of people coming in boats in large numbers and drowning. They said nobody will qualify as a refugee if they come through this route, but we will process people offshore genuinely and sincerely; and if they are people who because of their race, religion, or political beliefs qualify as refugees, we in Australia will have them. Wouldn't it make more sense, Louise, rather than having an open door to the Greek islands, to process people in North Africa and the Middle East?

RUDYARD GRIFFITHS: Now we're going to move on to the moderated portion of this discussion. We'll get into some of the issues that have been raised to date. It's been a hot exchange so far and I want to give Louise and Simon an opportunity to respond to the latest rebuttals we've heard. And Louise, because you were mentioned last by Nigel, let's have you respond first — and maybe specifically to this idea of whether Australia, with a very different approach than what's happening in Europe, is a model that should be considered.

LOUISE ARBOUR: Well, Nigel, it will come as no surprise to you that I can't think of much that I would agree with you two on tonight. This is not one of them. Australia is hardly a model of compliance with the Refugee Convention. Let's assume that we have a genuine asylum seeker as opposed to a gang rapist. Just for the sake of argument, let's start with a neutral proposition — somebody's knocking on the door. The Refugee Convention assumes that this asylum seeker will have to flee his or her territory probably by non-legal means. That's why we have irregular people. They often enter with no documentation because there are no open channels for these people to escape their predicament. The duty on the country of transit or destination is to have a fair and humane process to determine the bona fides of the refugee claim. Australia exports that responsibility — in the same way that the United States exports the responsibility to Mexico, not on refugee issues, but in its processing of migrants who come from Latin America. This is not the way to do it. Countries should receive people on the assumption that they may very well be people fleeing persecution. They should put in place a fair process in their country, particularly rich countries like ours, like Australia, like the U.S., who have full capacity to do so in a very decent, humane fashion. And, unfortunately, that's not the example that Australia has set out.

NIGEL FARAGE: But how does Greece cope with everything? Isn't this the point? I know that some people have gone to Italy, but Greece has seen just a vast influx of people and there is no sign of it stopping. A so-called deal with Turkey has seen routes from Libya opening up again. Of the million people who came through the Greek islands last year and finished up settling in Germany, virtually none were properly processed and not one of them was security-screened. And I wonder, under the 1951 definition of refugee status, how many of the million that went to Germany last year would have qualified as refugees. Five percent? Ten percent maximum?

I understand there are dreadful things happening in North Africa and the Middle East. All I'm saying is that if we broaden the definition of what a refugee is, European countries will not be able to support this influx indefinitely. Last year it was 1.8 million. It'll be 1.8 million this year, and 1.8 million next year. In the end, the people simply won't accept it.

LOUISE ARBOUR: Nigel, there are 500 million people in Europe. You think Europe doesn't have the capacity? It's not the lack of capacity — it's the lack of political will, in large part because the entire public debate is poisoned by the kind of discourse that we've heard tonight. We're supposed to talk about refugees and you talk about gang rape.

RUDYARD GRIFFITHS: Hold on a second, let's —

NIGEL FARAGE: Of course there is room in our hearts for all of Europe to give people refugee status. We just want to know that they're genuine refugees and not people coming to do us harm. That's all we want to know.

RUDYARD GRIFFITHS: I want to bring Simon in on this and then I'll come to you, Mark.

SIMON SCHAMA: I actually don't disagree with you about the need for better screening. I just want to say, though, to Mark's fulmination, that it's an appalling slander, to me, to the Muslim religion, to imply that —

MARK STEYN: I never said the word *Muslim* in my fulmination. It was a Muslim-free fulmination.

SIMON SCHAMA: The implication was that if you've got a Muslim immigrant he — and this will be a "he," according to you — is bound to commit a sexual crime sooner or later. That seems to be a monstrous and grotesque falsehood about Muslim communities that have been settled for a long time now in Britain and the United States. Dearborn, Michigan, is not full of —

MARK STEYN: Well, I will give you a Muslim fulmination then. Muslim men are about one and a half to two percent of the population in Norway. They account for half of all the rape convictions in Oslo. There *are* differences there. There are cultural differences. And if you think about it —

SIMON SCHAMA: What is it about Islam that you claim is designed to make men brutal, sexual animals?

MARK STEYN: I'm not talking —

SIMON SCHAMA: And why, then, don't you want to deport all Muslims from Europe and the Western societies that —

MARK STEYN: Because I distinguish. You're a historian. You know as well as I do how many more Muslim men in the First and Second World Wars fought for king and empire than Canadians. Muslims have a long tradition of loyalty and service to the crown. They were getting Victoria Crosses for extraordinary courage on the battlefield a hundred years ago today during the Great War. You know that. What has changed is that we are no longer importing someone who has been to a Muslim school in India in 1948, 1949, someone who would have received an education not different by that much from a grade-schooler in Canada or in Scotland or anywhere else.

RUDYARD GRIFFITHS: You've got to tell us where you're going with this because you're losing me. What's the point?

MARK STEYN: I'm just establishing my non-Islamophobic bona fides.

RUDYARD GRIFFITHS: Consider it done.

MARK STEYN: But there is an issue here.

RUDYARD GRIFFITHS: Let's move back onto refugees, because this debate is about the refugee crisis. There are other dimensions and we'll continue to get into them. But I want to come to you and pick up a little bit on what Mark and Nigel have been saying, which is that certain societies are better at integrating people than others. Traditionally,

Canada thinks that it's done a pretty good job. The United States is called the melting pot. European countries often are not very good at integration. Therefore, is this a different kind of crisis? Is this time different?

SIMON SCHAMA: I suspect and I hope that we might have a bit of agreement with what I'm about to say. I think Europe has done a pitiful job at forthrightly defending the virtues and moral decencies and political traditions of Western pluralist, liberal capitalist democracy. Europe is essentially an organization managing the business cycle and hoping for the best when it comes to shopping for Christmas. And that is an abject surrender. If we are ever going to make any headway against militant apocalyptic Salafism, there has to be something to offer the refugee population no matter where they come from. We need to be less defensive, less mute, less muffled. They should be reading Locke and Milton and Mill and making that tradition important and a stake in citizenship. Isn't it as important as screening and putting up walls and having decent counter-terrorist intelligence?

NIGEL FARAGE: I agree with you completely. We have been abject, pathetic even. We've lain prostrate on the floor. We've allowed people to come in, changed large parts of our communities and our cities, and nobody amongst our leadership — and this is not about getting religion in government — has had the guts and the courage to stand up for our Christian culture, because that's who we are.

SIMON SCHAMA: No, I don't want to hear "Christian," because I happen to be Jewish. There's nothing —

NIGEL FARAGE: Well, as you well know, it is a Judeo-Christian culture, all right? That is our culture today.

As soon as I start to talk about real values, you shrink into your shell like everybody else, don't you? We have a Judeo-Christian culture. We have been gutless and weak in defending it. Mark isn't suggesting that Islam's a bad religion, and I'm certainly not suggesting that either. But I am saying that Wahhabism, funded by the Saudi Arabians, has been a cancer within Islam, all right?

SIMON SCHAMA: I absolutely agree.

NIGEL FARAGE: The 1974 boom in the increase of oil has led to so much of what we're all suffering. Integration may have been difficult in the past, but here's why we're nervous and cautious about opening up our doors to untold millions of people from those countries today: never before have we had to live with the fifth column living inside our own communities and our own country that wants to kill us, blow us up, and change our way of life. I'm arguing for having a sensible refugee policy, but we must, must, must be able to screen people before they come to settle in our countries. Surely that's just plain common sense.

RUDYARD GRIFFITHS: I'm going to come to Louise on this point, and then I'll go to you, Mark.

LOUISE ARBOUR: We have to be very careful not to exaggerate the sense of danger and fear that this idea of infiltration can generate. It's a trap.

I've said this a million times, but if we had assumed that most Italians coming to this country, for instance, would be members of the Mafia or that most Asians would be members of the Triad, we would have closed the door. There is no basis upon which to suggest that the people who are fleeing the atrocious events in Syria, in Libya — and in northern Iraq and so on — are missiles that are being sent to infiltrate our communities.

You know what? I really believe that it's part of a very sophisticated strategic plan, by those who are intent on destroying our democracies, to tease us into an irrational response where we will destroy the very values we believe in. We will over-securitize and inevitably use security measures in a discriminatory fashion, with carding and racial profiling and so on. Slowly, we will destroy our very values out of sheer fear. We're going to do it to ourselves if we cultivate this culture of fear with overreaction, restriction on freedoms, over-securitizing, and targeting of these vulnerable minorities rather than protecting them and including them.

MARK STEYN: We are getting to the meat of it now. People talk about European, British, and Canadian values without ever defining them. And I think Simon is right that it's not just about car-chase movies and rap songs and all the rest of it. There's something underlying. I share Louise's fears of the big security state entirely because I like to write and say what I want, and my writing wound up in front of three human rights commissions in Canada. So I certainly don't want to see the Europeans erect a bigger security state with less free speech than Canada. I would hate to see that.

Here's the reality of the situation: look at what happened with the *Charlie Hebdo* slaughter in Paris a year ago, and then look at the polls of the Muslim communities afterwards. They don't want to put a bullet in a cartoonist and they don't want to blow up the Brussels airport, but there is no commitment to the traditional Western understanding of free speech. And as Simon says, we don't teach them it. We don't assimilate them. You have to have an assimilation tool because if you don't, you end up with bicultural societies such as Bosnia, which Louise dealt with. Bicultural societies are always fundamentally unstable — sometimes more or less benignly so, like Northern Ireland, and sometimes more dangerously, like in Rwanda, as Louise can tell you. But if you don't assimilate these people coming into Europe, then you will have bicultural societies and they will tear Europe apart.

LOUISE ARBOUR: Mark, I assume it's been a long time since you've lived in Toronto. Is that a fair assumption? Have you seen street signs in languages you can't understand? This is the city *we* live in. We're not scared.

MARK STEYN: I was born in Toronto. I've been away for a couple of years. You're from Quebec, so you know as well as I do that the differences between Quebec francophones and Ontario anglophones are footling in the scheme of things. Yet twenty years ago a majority of your fellow Quebec francophones voted that they didn't want to be in the same country as these guys. You're trying to tell us that Germany or Sweden or Molenbeek — the Islamic emirate inside of the kingdom of Belgium. Twenty-five percent of the population of Brussels is Muslim — will somehow be more fundamentally stable and secure than Northern Ireland?

LOUISE ARBOUR: I lived in Belgium, in Brussels, for five years until recently. They don't have to wait for people coming out of Molenbeek to have separatist tendencies.

MARK STEYN: My mom's Flemish. I know that.

LOUISE ARBOUR: Exactly.

NIGEL FARAGE: Well, England's fairly united. Scotland not always, I would agree! But Mark's point is very interesting. Within England we are seeing the growth of a parallel society: 80 percent of Muslim marriages in Britain are not recognized under U.K. law. They're conducted under Muslim law, which gives the women far fewer rights than they would have under U.K. law. We now have eighty-three sharia courts in England. We now have tens of thousands of cases of female genital mutilation taking place every single year in England. We think of England as a country with problems that aren't as big as some of the others in the EU, and yet there's not yet been one prosecution within our system.

So Simon and I have got some degree of agreement on this issue: the law has to be applied equally to everybody. We mustn't be scared of applying the law equally to ethnic minorities. If we are, we're stockpiling massive problems for the future.

And Louise, I'm sorry. You're trying to compare some of the concerns that we've got on this side of this debate with previous migrations. You used the word *exaggeration*. Well, it's not an exaggeration unless you think the boss of Europol is wrong. Should we be concerned when he tells us there are five thousand jihadists/terrorists that have come into Europe in the last eighteen months through the Greek islands posing as refugees? Should we be concerned? You bet your life we should be concerned. Only eight of those terrorists killed 130 people in Paris. We have a problem here. Get out of denial, please.

SIMON SCHAMA: The deep problem is that jihadi cells exist. The San Bernardino shooting was a case in point. The main shooter at San Bernardino was an American citizen. His wife had a green card. A very significant number of those who are actually carrying out these appallingly homicidal conspiracies are British, American, French, and Belgian citizens. Now, I think we're agreed that this appalling degree of criminal negligence is partly because they're not noticing when somebody's deported from Turkey to the Netherlands and is known as a terrorist, particularly in the case of the Belgian authorities. But if you're going to do something about homegrown Salafist jihadism, you have to engage with the Muslim community, not demonize it en masse. You actually have to welcome the work of the Quilliam Foundation.

NIGEL FARAGE: Yes. Well, I do.

SIMON SCHAMA: You have to start not from the pessimistic assumption that all Muslim immigrants or refugees are necessarily going to constitute a fifth column, but from the possibility at least that they can lead active, decent lives of citizens. I don't disagree with you about the horror of genital mutilation. Those should be prosecuted. We're with you on this.

NIGEL FARAGE: We already have a problem within our countries. What I am urging is that we don't have a complete open door to all the huddled masses so we make the problem even worse. That's the point of this debate.

SIMON SCHAMA: Absolutely. But that's already over. The EU-Turkey agreement is going to return vast numbers of migrants who land in Greece. Although, I want to say —

NIGEL FARAGE: And then let 77 million Turks join the EU and have free movement? It's hardly a victory, is it?

MARK STEYN: Simon's point is right, here. When you've got second- and third-generation Belgians, Frenchmen, Germans, Britons, and Canadians going off to join ISIL, blowing up Paris, blowing up Brussels, that should foster a certain modesty among us that our skills at assimilation are not as awesome and all-encompassing as they were in the nineteenth century. And to think, the response is to suddenly accelerate immigration from the same source? It's very bizarre. In what sense are these people Belgian?

SIMON SCHAMA: In what sense is Razia Iqbal British? She's fully British, right?

NIGEL FARAGE: Yes, she's fully British.

SIMON SCHAMA: And she happens to be a British Muslim, right? And how much more British can you get than doing the BBC World Service?

MARK STEYN: Yes. I work with Zeinab Badawi at Channel 4 in Britain. I've got no problem with that. But that's my point. Holding a passport does not make you Canadian. It does not make you Belgian and does not make you French.

LOUISE ARBOUR: What?

SIMON SCHAMA: I agree. I think this is the difference between us, actually. There are those of us who are possibly naively optimistic humanists, who think it is not impossible to be an orthodox Muslim and a good Canadian or a good Brit, and a good democrat at the same time. And for that you need to be involved and engaged in exercises of civic education, which make it clear that you *can* indeed go to a mosque for Friday prayers and still be a decent, democratically participating citizen. And I don't think this has actually happened. If you go to the mosque and the imam happens to preach the destruction of the society that you're living in, bloody well turn him in. Turn him in!

RUDYARD GRIFFITHS: Mark, do you want to respond?

MARK STEYN: That doesn't happen, unfortunately. If you look at the RCMP statistics of radicalized mosques you'll understand that all over this city and Montreal and Calgary and Edmonton and Vancouver there are any number of radicalized mosques where people just sit on their hands. I go back to my point, Simon — you have to have something for migrants to assimilate with.

SIMON SCHAMA: Yes.

MARK STEYN: The people in British schools haven't a clue about most of the history you know. They don't teach history in North American schools. My kids are in some school where it's called Social Studies and they do a little bit of it and it's always the same thing. Martin Luther King comes round like the Number 23 bus.

SIMON SCHAMA: I actually have a movement to abolish the term now.

MARK STEYN: Well, good for you. I'll sign that petition.

SIMON SCHAMA: I'll sign you up, yes.

RUDYARD GRIFFITHS: I want to move on to numbers, because that's a big part of this debate. Turkey has 2.7 million Syrian refugees; Lebanon has a million. Nigel, if you look at Great Britain in terms of legally settled Syrian refugees, we're talking almost infinitesimal numbers compared to your European counterparts. What do Britain, Canada, and the United States owe their European allies in terms of trying to relieve the pressure that you and Mark have diagnosed so acutely within their societies right now? What do we owe them?

NIGEL FARAGE: We have a newfound problem in the United Kingdom with this because we have an open door to half a billion people who are European Union citizens. As a result of that and generally a pretty weak U.K. immigration policy, net migration to Britain is running at a third of a million a year. That's if you believe the figures, which I really honestly don't.

So our population is increasing by a third of a million every year, ten times the postwar average. As a result, David Cameron has said he's going to accept twenty thousand Syrian refugees over the course of this parliament. I'm absolutely certain that if the United Kingdom had an Australian-style point system for immigration and we had net immigration running at average postwar levels of thirty thousand a year, we'd find room for some more genuine refugees. And I hope that when we did, we'd look at the plight of the Christians who are being massacred in Libya, Iraq, and Syria. Based on every definition that the United Nations has stood for since 1951, those Christians should be guaranteed freedom, security, and refugee status in the West.

I think Britain, Germany, and Sweden are actually becoming very hard-hearted because of the free movement of people. We're becoming rather hard-hearted to things that twenty years ago we'd have been happy to accept.

RUDYARD GRIFFITHS: Mark, the United States has a population of over 300 million, but only twelve hundred Syrian refugees have been legally and officially admitted into the country. Is the United States shouldering its burden of this crisis?

MARK STEYN: No, but they don't look at it from a humanitarian perspective on principle. They see it as part of the big security picture. And it's a little surreal to be holding this debate in the week following Brussels. Louise and Simon, I think, want to detach the general migration question from the terrorism question, and the Americans don't see it that way. I was glad to hear that the zealots of Canadian customs turned Simon over at Pearson earlier today. It's good to know there's always someone they don't want to let in the country! Immigration minister John McCallum is going to say, "We're not going to have the chaps committing the gang rapes. No, we're screening for them," but if you have ever had the pleasure of undergoing so-called secondary interrogation, as this suspicious character did earlier today, you will know that no Western government has a clue about who it lets in.

The person who committed the San Bernardino crime had a green card. She basically used a jihadist dating site to put together a terrorist cell. It was an arranged marriage for the purpose of committing terrorism. And she aced some sort of immigration test. It's all "money is no object" down south. It's not like here, where there's just one little agency dealing with it: the Canada Border Services Agency. They've got something like ninety-seven agencies south of the border looking at this woman. She aced five separate tests and she still got into the country. America takes the view that it has no idea who any of these people are and it's better to be safe than sorry.

RUDYARD GRIFFITHS: Let's come back now to you, Louise. What do Canada and the United States owe in terms of their share of this crisis?

LOUISE ARBOUR: I think we have to bring this debate a little bit back into a less apocalyptic scale. As I said at the beginning, the wording of the motion was a poetic way of capturing the spirit and the letter of the Refugee Convention. Now I think we've drifted into the movement of people who in fact are, for the most part, unregulated by international law or international treaty. What we're talking about now — this so-called huge crisis facing Europe — is very well defined by the Refugee Convention. But we haven't made a dent in talking about the millions of stateless people in the world who don't have a passport. And by the way, Mark, if you have a Canadian passport you're a Canadian citizen. There's no arguing with that, right?

We haven't made a dent in dealing with statelessness. We haven't made a dent in talking about what are called

IDPs, internally displaced persons, of which there are millions in Syria itself and in Sudan. These people are stuck in their own country against a predatory government. We have no framework to deal with them and to help them.

What we're talking about are people running away from oppression. And frankly, when you consider the immense risks they're taking to flee, we have to assume that at least the majority of them are bona fide refugee applicants. We simply have to process them. We're talking about very small numbers. Put millions into context: it's millions of refugees knocking on the door of a billion people, if you put Europe, North America, and all the capacity of the world's wealthy nations together.

The key, I believe, is international co-operation. There's no reason Greece, which was having a lot of financial problems itself, should have been stuck with bearing the largest burden. The European partners, and the Western countries generally, should have stepped up to the plate. I think Canada should still do so beyond the already generous signal that we have sent.

We have the luxury in Canada of doing a full pre-screening. People don't row into Canada. They sit in refugee camps where we have months and months of pre-selection processes through the UNHCR. With the luxury of these processes in place, we should be doing tons more, but that would require everyone to work in that direction and stop exaggerating. I'm not saying there are zero security risks. But I think it will be a stain and a shame on our generation if our response is to blow it up to such an extent that we start talking about erecting walls with barbed wires.

RUDYARD GRIFFITHS: We're coming to the end of our cross-examination period, but Simon, I want to give you the last word in this segment before we go into closing statements.

SIMON SCHAMA: I just really want to echo what Louise has said and quickly mention a piece of information that came out today in a report from Amnesty International. It casts a very long shadow over the Turkey-EU agreement, if that's going to happen. This very, very credible report states that Turkey has been forcibly deporting Syrian refugees back to the war zones from which they have come, which is a horrific thing to contemplate if it is true. The Turks have denied it, but there seems to be a very substantial amount of evidence to suggest the claims are correct. It throws the issue back to the place that we should have perhaps spent more time on, as Louise suggested. There is this kind of universe of misery and suffering, especially considering that one in every three displaced persons in these hellish camps in Syria, some in Jordan and Lebanon, are children, and we have to really think about their plight rather than obsess quite so much on jihadists and rapists in German cities.

RUDYARD GRIFFITHS: Very good. It's time now for closing statements. We're going to proceed in the opposite order of our opening statements. So Nigel, your three minutes will go up on the clock and you have a say.

NIGEL FARAGE: Well, thank you. And thank you for a very civilized debate. We started off with 77 percent against our side of the argument, which, compared to the odds

I'm against when I'm in the European Parliament, strikes me as being quite a good start.

I've tried to make the point that I do think it's beholden upon people in the West to open their hearts to genuine refugees, people who live in fear of direct persecution, imprisonment, and death because of their race, religion, political beliefs, and indeed, sexual orientation. I've tried to make that point, and I also have no doubt that America and Canada could do an awful lot more than they're doing when it comes to refugees. But it's Europe that has faced the front line of this issue over the course of the last eighteen months, and we have thrown out of the window our classical definition of what a refugee is and broadened it to include anybody coming from a war-torn area or, frankly, anybody coming from a poor country.

What Chancellor Merkel did clearly was irresponsible, damn stupid, and will cost Germany for many years to come. In the modern world we *do* have a genuine terrorist threat.

It's likely that we only need to be concerned about 3 percent of the Muslim communities that are coming into Europe, but if only eight people can cause all that misery we saw in Paris, and half a dozen can do what we saw in Brussels, we have to be careful. We need security checks. We have to process people offshore and make sure they're genuine refugees. And I've tried this evening to challenge the other side to see whether they would agree with me that the Christians who are being crucified and massacred in the Middle East should qualify for refugee status and I've not had one positive response from them on this at all. And this, ladies and gentlemen, is the point.

You cannot support this motion. It is idealized non-sense. It doesn't make sense. What we need to have is a sensible, proper, common sense refugee policy to help those who are in peril. To open up our doors the way Angela Merkel did is bad news for Germany and is bad news for the West. Stand up and stop such nonsense and oppose the motion, please. Thank you.

SIMON SCHAMA: I want to say I don't disagree at all with your point about the Christian community. The same goes for the Yazidis and Shia Muslims. As far as ISIL is concerned, Shias aren't Muslim at all.

I want to end with the words of a Christian, not mine, written in 1624. You'll all know some of them at least, I'm sure. They are from the Dean of St. Paul's, John Donne: "No man is an island entire of itself; every man is a piece of the continent, a part of the main; if a clod be washed away by the sea, Europe is the less, as well as if a promontory were, as well as any manner of thy friends or of thine own were; any man's death diminishes me, because I am involved in mankind. And therefore never send to know for whom the bell tolls; it tolls for thee."

RUDYARD GRIFFITHS: Louise, we're going to go to Mark first, and then you'll get the last word. Mark.

MARK STEYN: Those of us on stage and many of the more distinguished persons in the auditorium tonight lead privileged lives. We jet off to the European Parliament in Strasbourg or to BBC television studios or to the transnational bureaucracy in Geneva, and from thirty-thousand feet it's easy to think that what's going on below us is swell. We will never have to live in Molenbeek in Brussels or Rosengård in Malmö. We will never have to live in Bradford or Toulouse. We get to go to the nice places. And that should imbue us with a certain modesty when we come up with grand, utopian schemes that testify to what Simon called our naively optimistic humanism. Down there in Molenbeek and in Rosengård they have to live with the consequences of our naively optimistic humanism.

We are striking attitudes. Simon spoke earlier about his Kurdish newsagent who's always a very decent chap when he hands him the *Jewish Chronicle* in the morning. We all know people like that. But at the same time, the political class is designing a solution to the great migrations of the world that will only end in tragedy, and I ask you not to vote for it. The more failed states that stay that way will only lead to more failed states in the future. Ultimately, it is better for Syrians to be able to live in Syria, for Afghans to be able to live in Afghanistan, and for Iraqis to be able to live in Iraq. The more beacons of liberty around the world the better.

I confess: I've never liked the Emma Lazarus poem that is stapled to the bottom of the Statue of Liberty. The French gave the Americans a fabulous statute and the Americans nailed a third-rate poem to it and turned it into a celebration of mass migration. Liberty and mass migration have nothing to do with each other, and often, the latter can imperil the former, which is where Simon's naively optimistic humanism may take us. We cannot fix failed states by inviting millions of their people to move in with us. All that ensures is more failed states and more disappointment. Eventually, one by one, the nations of the West will join them, and then you'll really be yearning to breathe free and there'll be nowhere to do it. Please vote against this motion.

RUDYARD GRIFFITHS: Ms. Arbour, you'll have the last word.

LOUISE ARBOUR: Let me say at the outset that I don't know of any evidence that suggests that Christians from Syria, or the Druze, or the Alawites, have been excluded from refugee protection. I don't know where this is all coming from.

What is being portrayed as a unique case in this debate tonight is in fact just another manifestation of the old myths, stereotypes, and prejudices that have met virtually every wave of immigration, and it's particularly odious when it targets refugees, not just any other kind of migrants. In fact, Doug Saunders in his book and in a piece that he wrote in the *Globe and Mail* made the point that many of the things that we hear today about Muslim refugees penetrating our Western societies with a fifth column intent on destroying it were also attributed, sometimes in relatively recent parts of our histories, to Catholics. For instance, they were said to be backwards and believed to have a loyalty to Rome more than to their home country; they lived in poor, crime-ridden neighbourhoods; and they were considered anti-democratic, authoritarian by disposition. Doesn't that sound also like the yellow peril? People thought we were all going to be transformed into a different society, and that we'd all end up being a mixed colour if we let in these millions of people from all over the world. This plays into exactly the same stereotypes and myths that we've heard at every single point in history.

The reality is that, despite an original knee-jerk, at times very hostile reception to newcomers, the history in this country has been a history of immense success of integrating people coming from all kinds of different cultures and religion. And integration is a two-way street. It has changed us historically and will change us in the future. We must have a very impoverished confidence in our democracy to think that it is so fragile that it cannot sustain the profound differences that will challenge our devotion to free speech, freedom of assembly, and pluralism. Thank you.

RUDYARD GRIFFITHS: Well, ladies and gentlemen, it was a hard-fought debate tonight, which brings to mind something that our founder, Peter Munk, has said on many occasions: it's one thing to get up, give a speech, and have the stage for forty-five minutes or an hour, but what we've seen tonight is something very different. Four big thinkers challenged each other, put their ideas out there, and contested this important issue. So please join me in a show of appreciation for a phenomenal debate. Very well done, and thank you.

Let's take a look at where public opinion was in this hall at the beginning of the evening: 77 percent of you agreed with the motion and 23 percent were opposed. Then we asked how many of you would be open to changing your mind, and 79 percent said you would be. It's going to be fascinating to see how all of you vote now based on what you've heard tonight from the "pro" and "con" sides.

I want to end by thanking the Aurea Foundation again for staging these phenomenal debates. They're a great addition to the city and to the country, and this evening has been available to people from coast to coast in Canada and across the continental United States.

We're going to do this all again next autumn, but in the meantime keep watching, keep learning, and keep reading. Thank you for joining us at the Munk Debates.

Summary: The pre-debate vote was 77 percent in favour of the resolution, 23 percent against it. The final vote showed 55 percent in favour of the motion and 45 percent against. Given that more of the voters shifted to the team against the resolution, the victory goes to Nigel Farage and Mark Steyn.

Pre-Debate Interviews with Rudyard Griffiths

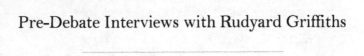

MARK STEYN IN CONVERSATION
WITH RUDYARD GRIFFITHS

RUDYARD GRIFFITHS: Welcome to our pre-debate interviews. We're having conversations with each of our debaters before tonight's confab on the global refugee crisis.

It's my pleasure to be sitting down with Mark Steyn. We know him as a celebrated columnist and a big media personality both here and in Canada and the United States: Fox News, the *Rush Limbaugh Show* — you name it, Mark's on it. He's also a bestselling author and a much-followed recording artist, which is terrific, Mark.

It's great to have you here and part of this conversation. What is a refugee in your view, and how does that relate to the debate we're having tonight?

MARK STEYN: A refugee is someone who has genuine fear of persecution. There are grave risks to genuine refugees, of whom there are many in the world.

Look at what's happened to the Christians in Iraq or the Yazidis: they have a genuine fear of persecution — a genuine fear of extermination.

But there are also people who just want to live in the West. If you can recall, there was a German village in Lower Saxony — I think it was Sumte — which had 102 people, and the German government said that they should take 750 refugees. They initially told them to accept one thousand and then downgraded it to 750.

Interestingly, that's roughly the proportion of the developed world to the rest of the planet. There are one billion of us who live in the developed world, give or take, and about six billion who don't. And not a terribly large proportion of them have to come to the developed world to completely overwhelm it.

The head honcho at Davos said a couple of weeks ago that he thought that a billion people were ready to make the move from the rest of the world to the developed world, essentially because Angela Merkel hung a sign out saying if you can get here, you can stay here.

RUDYARD GRIFFITHS: How would you respond to the argument that Syria is a failed state? There is mass death unfolding and there are a variety of people responsible for that, from Assad to various splinter and jihadist groups, and arguably we, the West, who have had no small role to play in this collapse. So, in a sense, what do we owe the people of Syria?

MARK STEYN: I think that's a good point and I accept that argument, although not in the case of Syria. I think it's certainly true in Iraq and Afghanistan. If Afghans are stampeding for the exits as a result of essentially an American protectorate for fifteen years, that's a poor reflection on Washington and the rest of the West.

But Assad and Syria, I think, is a slightly different case. But what is the best way to deal with that, as failed states multiply across that region and beyond? Do we simply import their populations and add them to ours?

I don't think so. I'm basically a nineteenth-century imperialist — a hundred years past my sell-by date, but my view is that I would prefer us to be in the business of exporting liberty rather than importing people.

The best thing we can do for Syrians is to enable Syrians to live in Syria, and enable Libyans to live in Libya, and enable Afghans to live in Afghanistan. The scale of these great migrations is potentially unlike anything the world has ever known.

RUDYARD GRIFFITHS: As a much-followed American conservative, you're someone who believes fundamentally in the values of individual liberty, the freedom of the individual, and the importance of open societies. Why do you think that kind of Western political thought isn't capable of successfully assimilating people who are coming from different cultures with different mores and views?

MARK STEYN: Well, I think that ideology can certainly assimilate them to a degree. I said I was an imperialist, and the British successfully exported those ideas around the world, which is why people would rather live in Barbados than Haiti, and they'd rather live in Malaysia than Indonesia. We can go all around the map and make those same comparisons.

However, I do think bicultural societies are almost always fundamentally unstable because one population is on its way down and one is on its way up. Madame Arbour knows a lot about this from her work in both Yugoslavia and Rwanda.

That's essentially what you have in continental Europe: countries that were hitherto ethnically homogenous nation-states have now imported another population from the other side of the planet. Just think of where the participants in tonight's debate come from — you've got two from the U.K. and two from Canada.

In the grand scheme of things, there's an absolutely minimal difference between the francophones of Quebec, where Madame Arbour was born, and the anglophones of Ontario, where I was born. The differences are insignificant.

Yet a majority of Madame Arbour's fellow Quebec francophones voted in 1995 that they didn't want to be part of the same country as you. In the U.K., the differences between Ulster Catholics and Ulster Protestants are, in the grand scheme of things, absolutely minimal. Yet thousands of people died in Simon Schama and Nigel Farage's country because one of those groups did not want to be in the same country as the other group.

Angela Merkel understands this. When we had the financial crisis a few years ago in Europe, she understood that the real problem with Greece is not the Greek economy, but Greece's culture. The Greek people are not like German people when it comes to their working habits. And she understood at a certain level that you could not transform Greeks into Germans.

Yet she seems to think now that the magic soil of Germany is so powerful that once you plant Syrian, Afghan, Yemeni, Iraqi, and Somali feet on German soil, you can turn all these groups into Germans, when she knows you can't turn Greeks into Germans. That's a mad vanity.

RUDYARD GRIFFITHS: Let's talk about the great melting pot. You live in the United States, which is one of the most successful countries in the world in terms of integrating people into a Pan-American culture. Yet to date, I think only twelve hundred Syrian refugees have been officially settled in that country. Do you think that number is too low? Do you think it's appropriate? Do you think America, which has a population of 300 million, should be considering larger scale settlement?

MARK STEYN: I think there's a difference between what I would call the settler nations of the West — Canada, Australia, New Zealand, and the United States, which are genuinely multicultural — and Sweden, Finland, and Germany.

The Americans are looking at this issue from a security perspective. There's something slightly surreal in holding this debate the week after what happened in Brussels. For people like Madame Arbour, security and refugees are two separate concerns, whereas for me, they're not. In a way, they testify to the limits of the assimilationist impulse.

The Ellis Island model and Emma Lazarus's poem from the resolution came at a time when America, like Canada, Britain, and Australia, was much more confident about who they were and were willing to impose assimilation.

In the absence of that, you get Molenbeek in Brussels, which has effectively seceded; it's an Islamic emirate within the kingdom of Belgium. And certain numbers are not yearning to breathe free; they're yearning to impose an entirely different kind of society on that country, which is why they blew up the airport and the railway station.

The *New York Times* says these crimes aren't being committed by refugees, and that Belgians and Frenchmen attacked Paris and Brussels. It's one way of looking at it.

The other way of looking at it is that assimilation is such a failure in those areas that even second- and third-generation immigrants, who nominally hold passports from Western nations, are so unassimilated that they want to blow themselves up at the airport in Brussels.

Perhaps that should give us pause that there are limits to what we can do. It's easy to be sentimental about this. Think about Catholics. It's certainly true that in this very town, well within living memory, the Orange Order had a generally negative, condescending, and patronizing view of Catholics as primitives.

But even in the worst of the Fenian raids, we were not living in a situation of cross-community sexual assault, of complete contempt for opposing cultures. History does not always repeat itself, and the fact that you can assimilate eastern European Jews and Irish Catholics does not mean that taking a Pashtun goatherd and dropping him on a nude beach in Scandinavia is going to work out as well as previous models.

RUDYARD GRIFFITHS: Fabulous to hear from you. You also have a very lively online presence, so please tell our viewers about your terrific website.

MARK STEYN: It's Steynonline.com, and that's *Steyn* with a $Y — S\ T\ E\ Y\ N$, as in why do I have to listen to this guy talk all this right-wing lunatic stuff at me?

RUDYARD GRIFFITHS: Mark, fabulous. I really enjoyed our conversation. I know you're going to be terrific on the stage tonight and we look forward to more of it.

MARK STEYN: I'm looking forward to it too. Thanks, Rudyard.

NIGEL FARAGE IN CONVERSATION
WITH RUDYARD GRIFFITHS

RUDYARD GRIFFITHS: I'm very pleased to welcome to Toronto Nigel Farage, who's just got off the plane from the United Kingdom. He's a member of the European Parliament and he's also the leader of the U.K. Independence Party that received almost four million votes in the most recent British national election. Nigel, great to have you here. You're an important voice in this debate, and we want to hear a bit of what you have to say right now.

You've looked at this issue very much through a security lens. From your analysis, you have a sense that the wave of migration that we're seeing out of the Middle East into Europe and potentially into the United Kingdom represents a security threat. Can you unpack this for us?

NIGEL FARAGE: Sure, but can I start with the very basics?

RUDYARD GRIFFITHS: Yes.

NIGEL FARAGE: We've got this debate tonight that I've even titled *The Global Refugee Crisis*, but I think we need to begin by asking ourselves, What is a refugee? My family were French Protestants. Perhaps you could have deciphered that by my French-sounding name. They were being burned at the stake and having terrible things done to them. They were refugees when they came to Britain in the 1700s. In Britain, we took people from Russia, particularly Jews who were suffering very badly. And we took Jewish people from Germany and Austria. We took Ugandan Asians, when Idi Amin went absolutely mad and threatened to kill them all.

No country knows more about how to act responsibly with refugees than the United Kingdom. But a refugee is somebody who directly fears persecution because of their race, religion, orientation, or political views, all right? What we've had, really starting last April and May, coming across the Mediterranean into the Greek islands and a bit into Italy is a vast migratory wave of people, hardly any of whom qualify as refugees.

I do believe those of us in the West should have compassion in our hearts, and should be able to offer refugee status to people who are genuinely in fear of their lives because of who they are, but the European Union have completely redefined the meaning of refugee. They've said that you qualify as a refugee if you have been displaced by war, and, even more stupidly, if you come from a poor country.

So, by my calculations, that means about three billion people could potentially come into the EU. We've had an open door, and a million people settled in Germany alone last year. We have not been able to conduct proper security checks on a single one of them.

Here's the real problem, which explains why I'm focusing on security. I remember, as a little boy, watching the BBC News and seeing Ugandan Asian families on the tarmac at Heathrow who were humble, grateful, and saying thank you to Great Britain for giving them refuge because Amin was going to kill them. They said they were going to work hard and integrate. They wanted to become part of our community and society. And, by goodness me, they've been the most successful migrant wave that has ever to come to the United Kingdom.

What we now have are predominantly young, aggressive males who, when they cross the border into an EU country, punch the air and chant like football supporters. And not one of these economic migrants has been through a security check.

RUDYARD GRIFFITHS: Europe has severe demographic problems: they need younger, vital males to ensure professions are filled and so their economies succeed now and into the future. Not to mention, as you point out, the previous waves of immigration were reasonably successful. Europe has not had a history of failed immigration.

NIGEL FARAGE: But then there's a difference, firstly in numbers.

RUDYARD GRIFFITHS: Okay.

NIGEL FARAGE: When those Ugandan Asians came to Britain, there were only twenty-eight thousand of them. Legal migration into Britain last year was 600,000. We're looking at different numbers and a different scale than anything we've seen before. Here's the real problem: ISIL has said they will use the migrant crises to flood Europe with their jihadist fighters. Ever year I've been saying that perhaps we should listen to them. Three weeks ago the boss of Europol, the EU's own police force, said that he now believes there are five thousand jihadist fighters who've been engaged in the war in Syria and who've come into Europe posing as migrants. We have a real security issue.

RUDYARD GRIFFITHS: You also have long-standing allies from Europe who, unlike the United Kingdom or Canada, are not separated by a body of water, and are therefore not separated from this wave of migration by any obstacle. What do Canada, the United States, and the United Kingdom owe their European allies in this crisis?

NIGEL FARAGE: You're right that the borders in much of Europe tend to be slightly more vague than they are in the United Kingdom. We're an island, so it makes life a bit easier. But the EU has introduced this thing called Schengen, and Schengen means you can travel freely around Europe. The idea was fine and dandy, even wonderful. It lets nice people travel freely around Europe. The problem is it lets bad people travel, too. And there has been a big rethink going on, not amongst politicians, but amongst voters. The Kalashnikov rifles that were used to kill 130 people in the Paris massacre last November were transported from Berlin in the trunk of a car. They crossed the Dutch border into Belgium and then they got to France. At no point did anybody stop the car, ask the travellers for a passport, or do a check. Alternative for Germany, a very new party, which is surrounded by scare stories, got 25 percent of the vote the other day in an east German province; this shows that there is a big rethink happening.

What do we owe our allies? What do we owe our friends? The same things that we've always owed them: solidarity, friendship, and good advice. When Australia faced a similar problem of large numbers of people coming by sea to claim refugee status and drowning along the way — although, granted, it was not to the same extent as we've seen in the Mediterranean — the Australians said no. They said that anyone who comes by this route will not be given refugee status. If you want to apply to come to Australia as a refugee, we will process you offshore. That is what the Australians have done, and I would suggest that it is what the European Union now needs to do.

RUDYARD GRIFFITHS: Do you think this agreement with Turkey is a movement in that direction? Do you welcome it?

NIGEL FARAGE: Do you know something? The British prime minister has just renegotiated with the European Union

63

ahead of a referendum that we're going to have on our continued membership in that union, taking place on June 23. I wish the Turks had negotiated for us because we've agreed to give them six billion euros. We've agreed that we'll send some people back who aren't genuine refugees. In exchange they will send us people that they deem to be refugees. We will have visa free access for seventy-seven million Turks by July, and we've got Turkish membership in the European Union on fast track. Overall, in terms of migratory waves, the deal with Turkey has made things a lot, lot worse.

RUDYARD GRIFFITHS: This is a complicated crisis that, in many ways, has its origins in what's happening in the Middle East. There are now a series of failed states that stretch across that continent. How do you see this coming to an end? Is there responsibility, first and foremost, to sort out the crisis in Syria?

NIGEL FARAGE: I'm sorry, but we've caused much of the crisis.

RUDYARD GRIFFITHS: Indeed, I won't argue that.

NIGEL FARAGE: For more than fifteen years, I have been consistently saying that we need to stop meddling with Arab nationalist regimes. We may not like the men that run those countries, but they are at least secular, and that went for Gaddafi as well. It even went for Saddam

Hussein. I'm not praising these people, but I'm pointing out that we do bear some responsibility for what has happened.

I'm going to make one plea: there's one group of people that have been completely ignored in all of this and they're called Christians. The Christians are being massacred in Iraq and Syria. Their numbers are about a tenth of what they were twenty years ago, and despite this massive migrant crisis, no politician in Europe has said, Let's give refugee status to the Christians who've got nowhere else to go.

We're not thinking right. We do not understand the history of how to deal with refugees. I'm not cold-hearted, and I'm not turning my back on people in genuine need. I'm just suggesting that in terms of the global crisis, the European Union is the absolute worst example of how to deal with it.

RUDYARD GRIFFITHS: Nigel Farage, we look forward to hearing more of this tonight on the stage of Roy Thomson Hall.

SIMON SCHAMA IN CONVERSATION
WITH RUDYARD GRIFFITHS

RUDYARD GRIFFITHS: It's a real pleasure, frankly a personal pleasure, to welcome Simon Schama. He is a widely read historian and author. I've read a number of his books, like so many people, and enjoyed his thoughtful, nuanced, and textured analysis of history. He's considered one of the really important cultural commentators of our time, and he's also a professor now at Columbia.

Simon, thank you so much for coming to be a part of this debate. We thought it was important to have a historian here to give some context, because this is an issue that the media often treats *sui generis*, when in fact great migrations are an essential part of human history. Can you situate what we're seeing now in the context of recent history and European history?

SIMON SCHAMA: Well, they both offer important analogies. There's no doubt that we're seeing transhumans — which is a terrible word historians used to use in the 1960s, when I was growing up. Just to be clear, I mean transhumans, not transgender, which means millions of people being displaced, and trying to find a place to live. On the one hand, the long period of the collapse of the Roman Empire comes to mind, but it's much more reminiscent, really, of what happened in the 1940s.

Even in the period toward the end of the First World War, going through to the Greco-Turkish war, which was terrible — it's easy to forget how elastic borders were, and not in a good way — great empires collapsed. Nobody knew what nation-states really were, and the First World War caused horrific moments of interethnic violence. The League of Nations was partly founded to try to deal with that. That was renewed in the aftermath of the Second World War.

So, this is really quite like the 1940s, in a way. But in a way it's worse, only in the sense that it's sort of unexpected. From the beginning of the Second World War to the end, everybody had seen the horror of vast numbers of people on the roads. It doesn't mean they were prepared for how it would turn out, with huge numbers of Germans uprooted from Poland and other peoples in eastern Europe going the opposite direction.

There's almost nothing that shakes us anymore, not even a mother with a battered tiny suitcase and an even more battered four-year-old clinging to her. How long was it before people started yawning at the spectacle of small children washed up on the beach? I got taken to task on British television for saying it was okay to have an emotional reaction about seeing children drowning, as their hands left their parents' arms, and that was thought to be very un-British. Maybe. I don't give a toss if it is.

RUDYARD GRIFFITHS: You're here tonight in no small part because of the religious beliefs of the majority of the —

SIMON SCHAMA: Nigel Farage better be very learned on Salafism, or I'll have him for breakfast. You need to make the case that Salafism and Islam are the same thing, or at least need to know the difference between Wahhabism and Salafism, if you're going to open your mouth about this issue at all. I'm sure the two we're debating tonight are very scholarly about it and know, for example, all the good Muslims in the trenches, battling against the jihadi version of Salafism, but I'm not going to give the game away. Do you make the claim, in the most absurdly horrifying way, of saying every Muslim is a threat by virtue of being a Muslim; that every Muslim hides some ferociously intransigent urge to wage jihad and bring down the West? Or are you actually a bit more intelligently discriminating about it, in my view. As you see, I'm getting worked up already, which is not good for a hustle technique.

What's very important to remember is that exactly the same things were said about the migrants coming into America and, no doubt, into Canada at the end of the nineteenth and early twentieth centuries. We said they wanted to destroy the West, and that they were filthy and lived off garbage. We said they couldn't speak English, and that they harboured destructive intensions. And amidst the millions who were coming in, welcomed by the Statue of Liberty, were anarchists and revolutionaries. There was a series of bombings in 1919, and Wall Street was bombed in 1920. But did that stop the general principle of the liberal democracies being tough enough and strong enough and absorptive enough to take that on and survive?

RUDYARD GRIFFITHS: Just fifteen minutes ago, Mark Steyn argued that those liberal democracies were different then. They were more confident about their culture. They were more able to imprint a set of shared values. I guess from his conservative critique of contemporary societies being too relativistic and too valueless that —

SIMON SCHAMA: No, well, I don't agree quite with that. I agree with the essential point that we've done an incredibly cowardly bad job about saying what the rules of a tolerant pluralist liberal society have to be. I suspect there are plenty of things that he and I might agree on, which is bad news for your debate. We might both invoke John Locke. You don't tolerate the intolerant, which was said by Milton and then by John Locke. But it is incumbent on you to be extremely forthright in upholding those essential values at least in order to have something worth defending. You can't just do it as a defense.

RUDYARD GRIFFITHS: Right. Would you also agree with him that Europe, fundamentally, does not have a successful multicultural model, and therefore is unable to integrate large numbers of non-Europeans?

SIMON SCHAMA: No, I think Britain did an amazing job, until Salafism came along. Turn on the radio in the morning and tune into the *Today* program. One of the first voices you'll hear is Mishal Husain. And, you know, British football would be crap without, actually, all kinds of people from immigrant descent. My green grocer is a Kurd. My newsagent's name is Ahmed, and he always points out when I'm in the *Jewish Chronicle*. I'm not saying that Southall and Bradford were, you know, completely problem-free. If you think about it historically, things might have been worse. Britain got out of India, including Muslim India, quickly. France did not, and France's long, long war in Algeria, and its painful, tormented relationship with the Maghreb made that, I think, in the end, a much more difficult and savage kind of process.

RUDYARD GRIFFITHS: Where do you think this crisis goes from here? Do you think —

SIMON SCHAMA: It changes every day.

RUDYARD GRIFFITHS: Does Europe survive this?

SIMON SCHAMA: I don't know. That's a very good question. There are so many things wrong. I'm actually in favour of remaining in Europe, still have my British passport there, though I live in New York. Europe has to find some sort of identity that is more than simply managing a business cycle. It needn't have the Founding Fathers gathered at Philadelphia, but something has to happen. It seemed to be happening with Angela Merkel's naive but magnificent hospitality, and then suddenly it was all a mistake and we had fortress Europe, and we had the Danes — the Danes! — taking jewellery off peoples' throats as collateral for their right to stay. It is in a desperate place, I think. So I don't know the answer to that. It's a big test. It's a big moral test.

RUDYARD GRIFFITHS: Do you worry about the rise of the far right? We've seen recent gains in Germany in the state election.

SIMON SCHAMA: It's been happening in countries like Hungary with Jobbik. Marine Le Pen is way ahead of potential opposition in the presidential polls, which is terrifying. I wish people wouldn't always Nazify it, really. Authoritarian nationalism can be quite bad enough without having to be a clone of the Nazis. It's a bleak kind of place.

RUDYARD GRIFFITHS: Just finally, to tap into your larger sense of the warp and woof of history: Where does the larger crisis go? What happens to the situation in the Middle East and the blossoming of this series of failed states? Do you see the potential for additional waves of migration to come out of that area? Do you see a prolonged period of instability?

SIMON SCHAMA: It's not looking great from the orbiting satellite view. What's extraordinary is there are three great problems. One is the slow death of the planet, beside which everything else is very small potatoes. The second is the staggeringly expanding inequalities between north and south in the underdeveloped world, inside industrial societies, too. The third is something we didn't actually think was going to be a huge problem when we were growing up, which is how do you find living space for people who are not like you, without the obligation of oppressing or possibly murdering each other. It needs to be faced eloquently and with a good deal of moral strength and honesty, which I know isn't much of an answer. The United Nations is so supine about this, really. It would be interesting to hear what Louise has to say about it.

RUDYARD GRIFFITHS: Simon … look, I've always wanted to interview you. I've now had the opportunity to do that, so thank you for allowing me to check something off my bucket list.

LOUISE ARBOUR IN CONVERSATION
WITH RUDYARD GRIFFITHS

RUDYARD GRIFFITHS: My guest is Ms. Louise Arbour, well known internationally and here in Canada. She's a former Supreme Court justice and UN Commissioner for Human Rights. She was also a chief prosecutor at the International Criminal Court at the Hague for the tribunals for Rwanda and Afghanistan. I could go on and on, but this is important. She's also CEO of the International Crisis Group, one of our most distinguished international non-governmental organizations.

Louise, thank you so much for coming to Toronto to be part of this debate.

LOUISE ARBOUR: Thank you.

RUDYARD GRIFFITHS: You have a legal background, and I'm wondering if you could start by framing this debate within that context. Emotion has driven a lot of our response to what we're seeing in Syria and what is unfolding in Europe. We have you here tonight in part to bring in that legal analysis.

LOUISE ARBOUR: Well, I'm glad you put it that way because I really think this is the proper framework within which we can start examining an issue that is really quite a challenge. A lot of people say this refugee flow is unprecedented, at least since the Second World War. And we have to remember that the legal framework that is in place — the 1951 Refugee Convention — is a product of the lessons learned from the disastrous lack of management of the flow of refugees, immigrants, and people on the move during the Second World War. So this is, I think, the appropriate way to look at it.

RUDYARD GRIFFITHS: Have you been surprised at the extent to which that legal argument seems to have been lost in much of the public debate that we've had so far?

LOUISE ARBOUR: First of all, I should distinguish between Canada and other countries. I don't know if people say it jokingly, but they often describe Canada as the only country in the world where you can actually win an election on a pro-immigration platform. And I think the last federal election in part confirmed that.

But I think, generally speaking, there's often a knee-jerk resistance to any kind of intake of foreigners, whether they are economic migrants who come in with money but raise the value of properties, at one extreme, to very impoverished refugees who come with nothing. Canada has invariably been transformed into a great success story because of immigration, so I think that's what we have to keep in mind.

In this particular crisis, there is a vigorous effort to try to pretend that this case is different, that these refugees — migrants — who are coming, particularly from the Middle East, are different. People are claiming they're not just a burden but an actual threat.

This is not new. When eastern European Jews were coming to Canada, a lot of the same types of things were being said: they're Bolsheviks and exporters of communism. Today there's this invidious discourse that all Muslims are terrorists. Even if they don't go that far, they say all Muslims are anti-democratic and incompatible with life in democratic society. This, I think, is what we have to push back against. It is factually wrong and morally repugnant.

RUDYARD GRIFFITHS: Right. Tonight I think we're going to hear the argument that Europe and the Middle East are, in a sense, two different civilizations. The civilization from the Middle East has a different set of views around the role of religion in society, the role of women, and the extent to which individual rights and freedoms should be extended or not. You feel that there's the potential here for these people to be successfully integrated over time into Western European culture. What about Germany, which is taking on hundreds of thousands of migrants?

LOUISE ARBOUR: Certainly everything in our history suggests that this should be exactly the case. It's certainly the case in Canada. Others can be the judge of whether Canada can export some of the mechanisms that have made that a success story. But I think the evidence shows that immigration has been a very positive force for development in the short term, medium term, and long term.

The only relevant question is whether this group is different. And as I said before, I think every time a group of newcomers come in, the assumption always is that these are the true scary foreigners, not like the ones before. There's no basis to suggest —

RUDYARD GRIFFITHS: Catholics, for example, you know, were an example of that. There was a lot of —

LOUISE ARBOUR: Absolutely, and in ways very similar to what is currently being said about Muslims. Doug Saunders from the *Globe and Mail* wrote really brilliantly on that issue. He showed that in some parts of Canada, Catholics were seen as backwards. They were thought to have very high fertility rates, and were ignorant supporters of authoritarian ideologies. Their neighbourhoods were often poor, crime-ridden —

RUDYARD GRIFFITHS: They were seen as disloyal. Their loyalties were to Rome, not to —

LOUISE ARBOUR: Exactly. They had a loyalty that was fed by the intensity of their religious views, which people thought could alter their democratic values. You hear that today and you want to laugh, and yet it's exactly this bundle of stereotypes that we hear being peddled today.

RUDYARD GRIFFITHS: This debate unfortunately happens in the aftermath of the terrorist attacks in France and now Brussels. I'm sure your opponents will say tonight that you can't have compassion without security, and that by allowing large numbers of migrants into countries, like Belgium, which clearly have a lack of infrastructure when it comes to security is irresponsible and dangerous.

LOUISE ARBOUR: Yeah. I think they'll say that. Ironically, I think this plays right into the hand of the agenda of the small nucleus of violent jihadist groups, like Daesh and al Qaeda and its affiliates, to some extent. They are using very sophisticated, smart ways of attacking the West — by essentially making us self-implode, by forcing us through the tactic of these targeted killings in our capitals to scare us into abandoning all the trappings that have made us successful open societies.

More security will invariably be applied in discriminatory fashion against unpopular minorities through racial profiling and so on. So they are teasing us into doing exactly that — showing an ugly response to human misery.

So I find it very ironic that those who are the proponents of these doctrines of exclusion are playing right into the hands of what will do more harm to democratic values and to democratic societies in the long term.

RUDYARD GRIFFITHS: And I guess you find a certain contradiction in these conservative voices, who are also supposedly proponents of individual liberty, of open societies, yet now seemingly embrace the apparatus of the security state to further that —

LOUISE ARBOUR: Exactly. You know the advanced arguments that have the trappings of rational, reasonable discourse. The bottom line is this is fuelled by ideologies of exclusion, racism, and hatred. So in a sense, I think what is animating their position is much more threatening to democratic values than the entrance of people into the country who may not yet share their values. If we're confident that the democratic model is the desirable one, why are we so concerned that we won't be able to make them embrace it when they have the benefit of living in pluralistic societies where children will be able to go to high-quality public schools, where they'll be exposed to other views? I find this ideology of fear and hatred much more dangerous.

RUDYARD GRIFFITHS: And I think it's important to note that the intelligence reports vis-à-vis the attacks in Paris and Brussels indicate that these terrorists were not migrants; these were alienated second- and third-generation citizens of these countries who —

LOUISE ARBOUR: That's true, but let's not be unduly romantic. Nobody ever said we should not take any Asians as immigrants because they could all be members of the

Triads, or that all Italians are in the Mafia. I mean, that's an overgeneralization.

The reality is that within a bunch of newcomers there will be, as there are in our own societies, all kinds of deviance, but it is usually in exactly the same kind of small numbers that we find in our own community.

I don't think we should obscure the reality. It's not all going to be easy and perfect, but it is clearly the right direction for us to take.

RUDYARD GRIFFITHS: Are you surprised at how many migrants are being accepted by countries that are not being forced to do so? I believe the United States has only settled 1,200 Syrian refugees, and they have a population of almost 300 million. The United Kingdom similarly has had very low official numbers of people settled. What do you think that says about the state of international awareness?

LOUISE ARBOUR: Well, I think it's immensely disappointing. As much as I think Canadians have been quite self-congratulatory because of all we've done well, we've still done only a fraction of what we should do in this particularly intense challenge to our friends and allies. We are the product of our geography. The chances are low of hundreds of thousands of people rowing into Canada or literally walking across the border, although some suggest that the upcoming American elections may change that. Let's not go there yet.

The reality is that we are immune to the kind of management crisis that this kind of migration poses. I think it puts an additional burden on us to be good friends to our friends who don't have the same luxury as we have to do pre-screening through resettlement programs administered by the High Commissioner for Refugees in Jordan and in Lebanon. It allows us to pick and choose and to host families in the best possible conditions in an orderly fashion.

We have to feel for our friends like Germany, and I think we should be extending a hand to relieve the pressure on Turkey, Jordan, Lebanon, but also on the Europeans who don't have the luxury of these more orderly mechanisms.

RUDYARD GRIFFITHS: As a jurist and someone who's considered these issues a lot, what do you think of the current European agreement with Turkey. It will allow Turkey to return migrants who have crossed into their country and then send them back into Europe on a one-to-one basis, provided that they've been screened at refugee camp based in Turkey. There are some questions as to the legality of this.

LOUISE ARBOUR: Yeah, and I hate to advance legal opinion. I haven't scrutinized the details of the arrangement, but the mechanism is not dissimilar to what the United States is doing by pushing back the burden on Mexico, for instance, to interfere with the flow of immigrants that come from Honduras and Guatemala. It's the same kind of principle, which the Australians have perfected. Exporting your obligations in an international framework is not really admirable, I think.

Germany in particular, Europe in general, and Turkey are all at the forefront of the management of this crisis.

I'm not hugely impressed with that particular mechanism, and I think we should be very alert to the danger of that, of pushing the burden back on those who have even fewer means of dealing with the issue.

RUDYARD GRIFFITHS: Ms. Arbour, thank you for coming to Toronto. It's going to be a privilege to hear you speak tonight. And again, thank you for accepting our invitation.

LOUISE ARBOUR: Thank you for having me.

ACKNOWLEDGEMENTS

The Munk Debates are the product of the public-spiritedness of a remarkable group of civic-minded organizations and individuals. First and foremost, these debates would not be possible without the vision and leadership of the Aurea Foundation. Founded in 2006 by Peter and Melanie Munk, the Aurea Foundation supports Canadian individuals and institutions involved in the study and development of public policy. The debates are the foundation's signature initiative, a model for the kind of substantive public policy conversation Canadians can foster globally. Since the creation of the debates in 2008, the foundation has underwritten the entire cost of each semi-annual event. The debates have also benefited from the input and advice of members of the board of the foundation, including Mark Cameron, Andrew Coyne, Devon Cross, Allan Gotlieb, Margaret MacMillan, Anthony Munk, Robert Prichard, and Janice Stein.

For her contribution to the preliminary edit of the book, the debate organizers would like to thank Jane McWhinney.

Since their inception, the Munk Debates have sought to take the discussions that happen at each event to national and international audiences. Here the debates have benefited immeasurably from a partnership with Canada's national newspaper, the *Globe and Mail*, and the counsel of its editor-in-chief, David Walmsley.

With the publication of this superb book, House of Anansi Press is helping the debates reach new audiences in Canada and around the world. The debates' organizers would like to thank Anansi chair Scott Griffin and president and publisher Sarah MacLachlan for their enthusiasm for this book project and insights into how to translate the spoken debate into a powerful written intellectual exchange.

ABOUT THE DEBATERS

LOUISE ARBOUR'S career of public service includes sitting on the Supreme Court of Canada from 1999 to 2004, acting as the chief prosecutor for the International Criminal Tribunals for the former Yugoslavia and Rwanda, and serving as the United Nations High Commissioner for Human Rights. From 2009 to 2014 she was CEO of the renowned International Crisis Group. Arbour is a Companion of the Order of Canada and the recipient of twenty-seven honorary degrees. She is currently a jurist in residence at Borden Ladner Gervais LLP.

SIMON SCHAMA is an internationally acclaimed historian, political commentator, and art critic. He is University Professor of Art History and History at Columbia University, and the award-winning author of seventeen books, including *Rough Crossings* and *The Story of the Jews*. He is also the writer-presenter of fifty documentaries of art, history, and literature for BBC2 and has written and presented more than thirty television documentaries for PBS, the BBC, and the History Channel. He is currently working on *Civilizations*, a television history of world art.

NIGEL FARAGE is the leader and founding member of the U.K. Independence Party (UKIP). In the 2015 U.K. general election, the U.K. Independence Party came in third with 13 percent of the popular vote or 3.8 ballots cast. Mr. Farage was recently named "Briton of the Year" by *The Times* and ranked first in the *Daily Telegraph's* Top 100 most influential right-wing politicians. Since 1999, he has been a member of the European Parliament for South East England.

MARK STEYN is an internationally acclaimed author, writer, journalist, and conservative political commentator. He has written five books, including *America Alone: The End of the World as We Know It*, which was a *New York Times* bestseller. His commentaries on politics, arts, and culture appear regularly in the *National Post*, the *Wall Street Journal*, and *The Atlantic*. He guest hosts Rush Limbaugh's top-rated talk radio program and *Hannity* on Fox News television.

ABOUT THE EDITOR

RUDYARD GRIFFITHS is the chair of the Munk Debates and president of the Aurea Charitable Foundation. In 2006 he was named one of Canada's "Top 40 under 40" by the *Globe and Mail*. He is the editor of thirteen books on history, politics, and international affairs, including *Who We Are: A Citizen's Manifesto*, which was a *Globe and Mail* Best Book of 2009 and a finalist for the Shaughnessy Cohen Prize for Political Writing. He lives in Toronto with his wife and two children.

ABOUT THE MUNK DEBATES

The Munk Debates are Canada's premier public policy event. Held semi-annually, the debates provide leading thinkers with a global forum to discuss the major public policy issues facing the world and Canada. Each event takes place in Toronto in front of a live audience, and the proceedings are covered by domestic and international media. Participants in recent Munk Debates include Anne Applebaum, Robert Bell, Tony Blair, John Bolton, Ian Bremmer, Stephen F. Cohen, Daniel Cohn-Bendit, Paul Collier, Howard Dean, Alain de Botton, Hernando de Soto, Alan Dershowitz, Maureen Dowd, Gareth Evans, Mia Farrow, Niall Ferguson, William Frist, Newt Gingrich, Malcolm Gladwell, David Gratzer, Glenn Greenwald, Michael Hayden, Rick Hillier, Christopher Hitchens, Richard Holbrooke, Josef Joffe, Robert Kagan, Garry Kasparov, Henry Kissinger, Charles Krauthammer, Paul Krugman, Arthur B. Laffer, Lord Nigel Lawson, Stephen

Lewis, David Daokui Li, Bjørn Lomborg, Lord Peter
Mandelson, Elizabeth May, George Monbiot, Caitlin
Moran, Dambisa Moyo, Vali Nasr, Alexis Ohanian, Camille
Paglia, George Papandreou, Steven Pinker, Samantha
Power, Vladimir Pozner, Matt Ridley, David Rosenberg,
Hanna Rosin, Anne-Marie Slaughter, Bret Stephens,
Lawrence Summers, Amos Yadlin, and Fareed Zakaria.

The Munk Debates are a project of the Aurea
Foundation, a charitable organization established in 2006
by philanthropists Peter and Melanie Munk to promote
public policy research and discussion. For more information, visit www.munkdebates.com.

ABOUT THE INTERVIEWS

Rudyard Griffiths' interviews with Mark Steyn, Nigel Farage, Simon Schama, and Louise Arbour were recorded on April 1, 2016. The Aurea Foundation is gratefully acknowledged for permission to reprint excerpts from the following:

(p. 51) "Mark Steyn in Conversation," by Rudyard Griffiths. Copyright © 2016 Aurea Foundation. Transcribed by Transcript Divas.

(p. 59) "Nigel Farage in Conversation," by Rudyard Griffiths. Copyright © 2016 Aurea Foundation. Transcribed by Transcript Divas.

(p. 67) "Simon Schama in Conversation," by Rudyard Griffiths. Copyright © 2016 Aurea Foundation. Transcribed by Transcript Divas.

Do Humankind's Best Days Lie Ahead?
Pinker and Ridley vs. de Botton and Gladwell

From the Enlightenment onwards, the West has had an enduring belief that through the evolution of institutions, innovations, and ideas, the human condition is improving. But is this the case? Pioneering cognitive scientist Steven Pinker and influential author Matt Ridley take on noted philosopher Alain de Botton and bestselling author Malcolm Gladwell to debate whether humankind's best days lie ahead.

"It's just a brute fact that we don't throw virgins into volcanoes any more. We don't execute people for shoplifting a cabbage. And we used to." — *Steven Pinker*

Should the West Engage Putin's Russia?
Cohen and Pozner vs. Applebaum and Kasparov

How should the West deal with Vladimir Putin? Acclaimed academic Stephen F. Cohen and veteran journalist and bestselling author Vladimir Pozner square off against internationally renowned expert on Russian history Anne Applebaum and Russian-born political dissident Garry Kasparov to debate the future of the West's relationship with Russia.

"A dictator grows into a monster when he is not confronted at an early stage . . . And unlike Adolf Hitler, Vladimir Putin has nuclear weapons." — *Garry Kasparov*

Has Obama Made the World a More Dangerous Place?
Kagan and Stephens vs. Zakaria and Slaughter

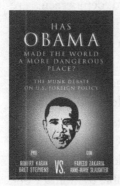

From Ukraine to the Middle East to China, the United States is redefining its role in international affairs. Famed historian and foreign policy commentator Robert Kagan and Pulitzer Prize–winning journalist Bret Stephens take on CNN's Fareed Zakaria and noted academic and political commentator Anne-Marie Slaughter to debate the foreign policy legacy of President Obama.

"Superpowers don't get to retire . . . In the international sphere, Americans have had to act as judge, jury, police, and, in the case of military action, executioner." — *Robert Kagan*

Are Men Obsolete?
Rosin and Dowd vs. Moran and Paglia

For the first time in history, will it be better to be a woman than a man in the upcoming century? Renowned author and editor Hanna Rosin and Pulitzer Prize–winning columnist Maureen Dowd challenge *New York Times*–bestselling author Caitlin Moran and trailblazing social critic Camille Paglia to debate the relative decline of the power and status of men in the workplace, the family, and society at large.

"Feminism was always wrong to pretend women could 'have it all.' It is not male society but Mother Nature who lays the heaviest burden on women." — Camille Paglia

Should We Tax the Rich More?
Krugman and Papandreou vs. Gingrich and Laffer

Is imposing higher taxes on the wealthy
the best way for countries to reinvest
in their social safety nets, education,
and infrastructure while protecting the middle class? Or does raising
taxes on society's wealth creators lead
to capital flight, falling government
revenues, and less money for the poor?
Nobel Prize–winning economist Paul
Krugman and former prime minister of Greece George
Papandreou square off against former speaker of the U.S.
House of Representatives Newt Gingrich and famed economist Arthur Laffer to debate this key issue.

*"The effort to finance Big Government through higher taxes is
a direct assault on civil society." — Newt Gingrich*

READ MORE FROM THE MUNK DEBATES —
CANADA'S PREMIER DEBATE SERIES

Can the World Tolerate an Iran with Nuclear Weapons?
Krauthammer and Yadlin vs. Zakaria and Nasr

Is the case for a pre-emptive strike on Iran ironclad? Or can a nuclear Iran be a stabilizing force in the Middle East? Former Israel Defense Forces head of military intelligence Amos Yadlin, Pulitzer Prize–winning political commentator Charles Krauthammer, CNN host Fareed Zakaria, and Iranian-born academic Vali Nasr debate the consequences of a nuclear-armed Iran.

"Deterring Iran is fundamentally different from deterring the Soviet Union. You could rely on the latter but not the former." — *Charles Krauthammer*

North America's Lost Decade?
Krugman and Rosenberg vs. Summers and Bremmer

The future of the North American economy is more uncertain than ever. In this edition of the Munk Debates, Nobel Prize–winning economist Paul Krugman and chief economist and strategist at Gluskin Sheff + Associates David Rosenberg square off against former U.S. treasury secretary Lawrence Summers and bestselling author Ian Bremmer to tackle the resolution, "Be it resolved: North America faces a Japan-style era of high unemployment and slow growth."

"It's now impossible to deny the obvious, which is that we are not now, and have never been, on the road to recovery." — Paul Krugman

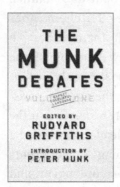